FIGHTING IS LIKE A WIFE

FIGHTING IS LIKE A WIFE

POEMS

ELOISA AMEZCUA

COFFEE HOUSE PRESS

Minneapolis

2022

Coffee House Press books are available to the trade through our primary distributor, Consortium Book Sales & Distribution, cbsd.com or (800) 283-3572. For personal orders, catalogs, or other information, write to info@coffeehousepress.org.

Coffee House Press is a nonprofit literary publishing house. Support from private foundations, corporate giving programs, government programs, and generous individuals helps make the publication of our books possible. We gratefully acknowledge their support in detail in the back of this book.

LIBRARY OF CONGRESS CATALOGING-IN-PUBLICATION DATA

Names: Amezcua, Eloisa, author.
Title: Fighting is like a wife : poems / Eloisa Amezcua.
Identifiers: LCCN 2021056125 (print) | LCCN 2021056126 (ebook) |
    ISBN 9781566896344 (paperback) | ISBN 9781566896428 (epub)
Subjects: LCGFT: Poetry.
Classification: LCC PS3601.M49 F54 2022 (print) | LCC PS3601.M49 (ebook) |
    DDC 811/.6—dc23/eng/20211119
LC record available at https://lccn.loc.gov/2021056125
LC ebook record available at https://lccn.loc.gov/2021056126

PRINTED IN THE UNITED STATES OF AMERICA

29 28 27 26 25 24 23 22   1 2 3 4 5 6 7 8

CONTENTS

FIGHTING IS LIKE A WIFE

Tale of the Tape

BOBBY CHACON		VALORIE GINN
November 28, 1951	DATE OF BIRTH	February 18, 1951
orthodox	STANCE	unknown
featherweight	DIVISION	spouse
Schoolboy	ALIAS	Val
September 7, 2016	DATE OF DEATH	March 15, 1982
64	AGE	31

EXCERPTS FROM A POST-FIGHT INTERVIEW: BOBBY CHACON
LIVES FOR TOMORROW

after Eve L. Ewing

A: I guess it's just the instincts of athletes against one another, you know, that comes into the picture, but I'm just a friendly guy. I ain't got nothing against not a single person, except myself maybe.

A: Being the oldest in the family, I was a little restless. I got restless & joined the gangs. I wasn't one of the biggest members so I had to prove that, uh, just the way I was [sic]. I had that thing where I had to be one of the best.

A: Yes, I should have.

A: There I was at 31 years old. How can a person that old throw that many punches?

A: I think it happened from that.

A: The only thing in the world I was afraid of was losing her.

A: & she had enough of me & she said, "No, that's it. Promise me," & I
        told her I couldn't keep that promise.

A: She did, she did. That's exactly what she thought.

A: That's right. I didn't care. I mean, I had everything I needed & then I
        lost it.

A: I've got a new life & everything's going real good right now & this is
        what I wanted. Now I've gotta go through with my career because she's
        gone.

A: You give up, you're out of the ball game. I don't give up.

A: This boxing is gonna be just like another marriage to me.

ROUND 1

You've taken punches like a man in the liquor store parking lot
& that time you checked out Eddie's girl for too long
when you drove from Pacoima with your friends
through hours of traffic to see the Venice boardwalk at sunset.
All the girls pretty in their short-shorts & bikini tops.
You gripped the blackjack in your pocket, knew you could beat Eddie
like Ali did Terrell, yelling *What's my name?*
But you let him hit you because you knew
the unspoken thing between a man in love & a woman is cruelty
—the pleasure of hurting someone other than yourself.

VALORIE

she's an ocean she fills the room

like water she is water she sways

like water she rocks as she sings

quietly she mouths the words

to her favorite song on repeat

again & again quietly one

wrong word & poof she might

unravel unspool there there

on her bedroom floor one

wrong step in any direction

one move & the wind she is

current she is air she moves

& the world at her feet

the world she is scatters

GOOD GAME OF CATCH

we

love

we're   going   to   play   a   good   game   of   catch

get

we   love   to   hit   back

got

two

fighters   love   a   game   to   play

who

love

to   play   we   fight   who   we   love

fight   fight

ROUND 2

One day, she was
not in your life.
Then there she was
with her long black hair,
smooth as Feliciano
singing *Come on,*
baby, light my fire.

TROUBLE

I was always
in trouble
with the police &
with the drugs
& always running
out in the streets
where you're
most likely to get
into trouble
I was always
with the drugs
& in trouble
with the police
& you're most likely
to get into trouble
where I always was
with the drugs
& the running
into trouble &
with the police
always where I was
with the drugs &
you're likely to get
the drugs
in the streets
& I was in
trouble always

VALORIE

because he keeps a knife in his pocket   his hands two fists

she hears he's used them

in the lot behind the football field he'll hit anyone who crosses him

friends say she ought to see him fight

a boy smiling he smiles when he strikes

she dreams of a kiss

the only fault she's found in him

is how he runs toward everything she fears

BLOOD

if you see it

down the side of my face

down the side of my face

leave me alone

if you see it

in my eyes

come take a look

blood out of your eye

it's difficult to rub the

& block left hooks

at the same time

ROUND 3

after Tyehimba Jess

Freedom is what you can buy
with a left jab & a right cross.

You've got the uppercut of a champ.
On a sweaty August night, you watch

Ramos v Ramos from the Olympic
on TV. You turn off the blaring AC,

want to hear the fighters' *tssiiuu tssiiuu*, exhaling
as they attempt to break each other's skin.

You're light on your feet like Mando,
got Sugar's hand speed. Freedom

is your girl by your side telling you to fight.
She brings your boxing license

in a lunch bag while you labor
at Lockheed, roots for you in Rocky

Lane's garage on a Sunday
as you spar any man who dares.

She wipes your burning face
with a cool towel, the sinewed shape

of your muscles surfacing quick
after you trade in Budweiser for a jump

rope. Freedom is the rattle in your jaw
the first time you take a hook

to the gut, the way a glove slides
across your nose slick with Vaseline

as you size up the weary contender,
know that look in his eyes that whispers

across the canvas between rounds. *Finish me
already,* body shriveling in the corner, *you've won.*

VALORIE

striking   with his enormous grin

& glossy shorts   his gloved hands

colossal   next to his boyish frame

Schoolboy   picks up his first win

her cheeks flush   the color of his knuckles

unswathed & tender   just now she wants

the soul   to figure out

between   the two of them

which one will be   the one

to break   the other's heart

FIGHTING IS LIKE A WIFE

it's with you
all the time
like a wife
it will know
if you don't
treat it right
but if you
treat it right
it can be good
like a wife
it's with you
all the time
you treat
her right
you know
if you don't
treat her right
a wife can't
be good
all the time
like fighting
like her
like a wife
the time
you don't
treat her right
can be all
the time
a wife can
be good
if fighting
can be good
all the time
you can fight

the wife
all the time
you can treat
her right
if you don't
treat her right
you will know
it can be good
fighting
it's good
good like her

ROUND 4

On the mornings you're home, you read
the newspaper over coffee.
That's what men do.
The National League won
the All Star game in Kansas City.
Germans bought a chemical plant
in Wyandotte, Michigan.
An officer in Dallas
played Russian roulette
in the front seat of a police cruiser
with his .357 Magnum & a 12-year-old boy
—Santos Rodriguez.
His older brother David
sat handcuffed in the back seat.
Under the headline, a photo of the boys
standing in front of a shiny car
taken months before the boy
became a headline.
They're beautiful & smiling
& you think of the picture
in the paper from the morning
before your fight with Olivares
—the two of you black haired
& tan skinned with your Mexican
surnames in bold letters overhead.
You could be brothers
even in the ring where he strafed you
with a straight right to the chin
so hard you fell to your knees.
He beat you unmercifully.
Ponce threw in the towel
between rounds & your undefeated
record gone. It's true
that brothers fight

& sometimes they bleed.
You read that the boys
were taken from their beds,
accused of stealing Cokes
from a vending machine.
The officer jumped out of the car
after the single shot hit Santos's head.
David told reporters
his baby brother's last words:
I am telling the truth
& how he reached with his body
yelling *you're gonna be alright*
as blood pooled on the car floor
until both of their feet were soaked.

VALORIE

baby touch   she touches her son

sleeping belly   smooth & warm

just eaten   ate from her breasts

the weight of mothering   leaves slowly

her body   he eats & she hears

in his throat a delicate swallow   beautiful song

stain leaking her body   the blood

still pooling   between her legs

rosy face   smiling baby in sleep

she made & unmakes   she whispers

into thin folds little ears   morning sun

the window   she hears the breeze & runs

her fingers across his head   close to hers

translucent skin   covered in dark, fine hair

just like his father's   what makes a person

so small so happy   it is a mere animal fear

that can only ask God   to keep life in her

THE MONEY

I don't care about the title
I'm in this for the money

~~I care about the title~~
I care about the money

~~I'm in this for the title~~
~~I don't care about the money~~

I'm for the money I don't care
~~I don't care I'm for the title~~

~~the title don't care about I~~
the money don't care about the title

I'm about the money
~~I'm about the title~~

I'm the money I care about in this

VALORIE

she asks him to quit   she sits

astride him   a kiss on the forehead

a kiss above his eye   gash

held together barely   layer paper-thin

she says to think   of the kids

thinks when they were kids   how she

got him into this   & again

she apologizes & again   she'll love him

the world is to be faced:

she knows   how to give

enough of herself   over as absolution

she knows   to keep asking

soon as the last debris   from the bleed

fades yellow   under skin

WE'RE HOPING

we're hoping I can win this fight
& the championship & three or four defenses
maybe I have enough money
I can put it into wise investments
& I'll be out of the game just like that
without the bruises & things that go with boxing

WE'RE HOPING

we're hoping I can win this fight
& the championship & three or four defenses
maybe I have enough money
I can put it into wise investments
& I'll be out of the game just like that
without the bruises & things that go with boxing

ROUND 5

You stride out of the arena, jump into your Morgan,
head to a club downtown, the gutters choked with headlines
from days before you were crowned the King of Los Angeles,
the City Champion; you've lied to your wife about where you're going—
you're supposed to be at dinner with the guys, friends who drink
your pockets dry, but there will be women, women who show you
their bodies bruised by men who think they're kings too,
skin soft as leather, faces that belong in magazines selling your wife concealer
or lipstick, the room reeks of too-warm whiskey & men's ambitions
YOU CAN LOOK BUT YOU CAN'T TOUCH
signs plastered on the walls, & the women, their legs float slow-motion
through the air—you know this weightlessness,
the way Little Red's body hovered over the canvas before crashing
a heavy thud, the crowd on their feet stomping a new song,
& now everybody in this town knows your name.

VALORIE

she searches her body

for the sight of   the wound

touches mouth   touches knee

arms outstretched   arms

bent   trying to get hold of

a shoulder blade   she can't find it

it must not exist   it must

be unreachable   inside

she wants to reach   inside

herself   she wants to swallow

herself   whole

SOME FINE WAY TO END A CRASH DIET

"He's so thin, I could wrap my arms around him two or three times."—Valorie

"All I can think about is hot dogs & root beer."—Bobby

I can't eat

I can't sleep

I'm dying of thirst

I can't stand it

I had nothing

my legs were gone

but I guess everyone could see that

couldn't they

?

ROUND 6: A LOT OF PLAY ON THE FACE OF BOBBY CHACON

Bobby

       bleeds badly

       bleeds from almost the first minute

       's in the ring like he's just happy to be here

       takes a great deal of punishment

       's face is a mess

       must find the center of the ring

       's legs aren't very sturdy

       fights with both hands & his chest

       looks sluggish

       's in trouble

       against the ropes

       strafed with a right

       's hurt

       goes down

       takes an uppercut like a champ

                             , you're the toughest guy I've seen

VALORIE

at each turn: his eyes, his figure,   —is it a dream or is it her own ill-desert—

    she watches the stars &   wants for nothing more   it makes no difference

everything is half unknown   that she is sure of   she looks to the sky

    she wants to be swallowed   whole, unmercifully   if only the world had

called her name   louder, if only her thoughts   were a little less rough

ROUND 7

A hit to the chin & you see
the black lights. Then you're driving

through the mall in San Fernando.
You think, *Where have I been?* & open

your eyes to the referee counting, slow
as honey glides through a jar:

Five. Six. Seven. His voice echoes
to no one but you. You have to get up.

The round's not over & you've got a thick
skull, learned early on you could take a punch,

absorb a man's fist in the brow or gut.
You rise but your legs stand still. You beg

your feet to dance their way away,
heavy hands to shield your face,

as the challenger charges toward you
like a tiger tasting blood.

BOBBY v VALORIE

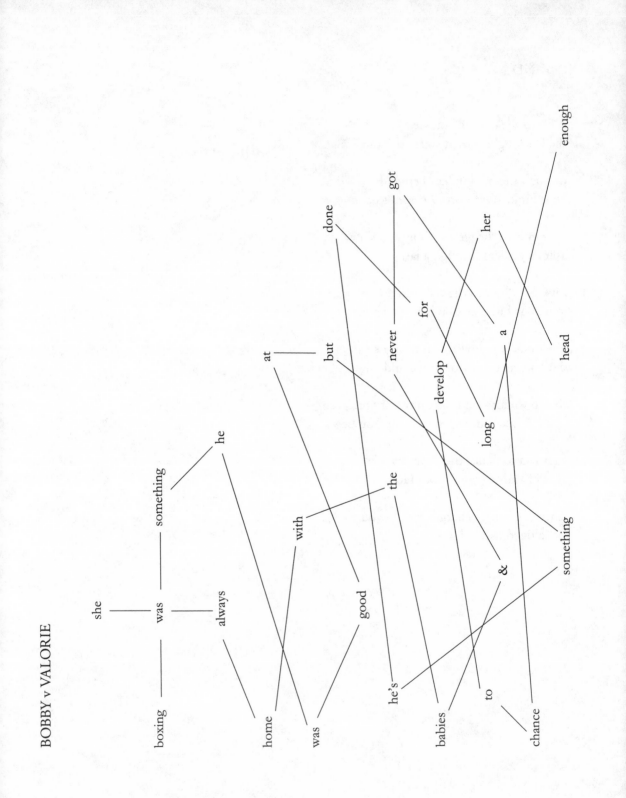

ROUND 8

after Mona Mansour

& now you're both in pain but you keep each other company in a way
& now you're both in pain but you keep each other company in a way
& now you're both in pain but you keep each other company in a way
& now you're both in pain but you keep each other company in a way

& now you're both in pain but you keep each other company in a way
& now you're both in pain but you keep each other company in a way
& now you're both in pain but you keep each other company in a way
& now you're both in pain but you keep each other company in a way

& now you're both in pain but you keep each other company in a way
& now you're both in pain but you keep each other company in a way
& now you're both in pain but you keep each other company in a way
& now you're both in pain but you keep each other company in a way

& now you're both in pain but you keep each other company in a way
& now you're both in pain but you keep each other company this way.

THE FACTS

why risk your life when things aren't going right   you have to face the facts   you have the rest of your life to live   if things aren't going right   you have to face the facts   why risk your life when things aren't going right   you have the rest of your life to live   if things aren't going right

ROUND 9: Addicted

to the *Bob-by! Bob-by!* as you emerge, robed & entouraged from your dressing room
to the feel of a man's fist crushing the bridge of your nose again
to the tang of dried blood on a mouthpiece
to the scent of beer & cheap cologne that fills the arena on a Saturday night
to the hiss of air leaving your opponent's lungs
to the touch of the ropes against your back holding you steady
to the blank in a fighter's eyes when you deliver a hook straight to the liver, right cross to the jaw
to the chill of the enswell on your cheekbone
to the bite of cold water swished in your mouth between rounds
to the smile on your trainer's face when the ring announcer calls a unanimous decision
   all three judges scored in favor of "Schoolboy" Bobby Chacon
to the prick of the needle stitching you back together
to the stench of sweat-stained wraps unfolding, falling to the ground

VALORIE

she lets a week go by the hours go by what   if she leaves   the pills there is a struggle

in her mind a gun she finds that she is not   there she doesn't know where there is the pills

she doesn't know

where she is a gun what has love done   for her what if she leaves finds herself there

what has love done the pills there   is struggle there in her heart there a gun

what love has done

for her she finds she isn't in her   mind the pills there struggle if she leaves

a month goes by   the hours go she leaves in her heart

a holy feeling

I SUPPOSE SHE THOUGHT I HAD SOMETHING GOING ON THE SIDE

she got mad
at the hospital
when she woke up   she ripped the tubes
& found out   out of her arm
she wasn't dead   & walked out   s h e d i s a p p e a r e d

s h e d i s a p p e a r e d   & walked out   she wasn't dead
     out of her arm   & found out
     she ripped the tubes   when she woke up
       at the hospital
       she got mad

ROUND 10

You call it love as you try to punch holes through each other
in the kitchen, no bell to force you to your corners.
Besides, her eyes, they'd follow you around any room—
this obsession, a fear she doesn't have a name for.

In your corner of the kitchen, she's a force
unlike any. Her voice rising, gradual as a balloon released into air.
Her fear, her obsession, a name she doesn't know yet.
You're out of practice. For weeks, you haven't been a husband

to anybody. Your voice rises & gradually, like a balloon releasing air,
you see her body tense, waiting for a counter
from a husband out of practice. For weeks, you've been
with another woman who asks where it hurts the most

when you tense your body waiting for a counter
in the ring. Tonight, you trade good punches near the end
where it hurts the most. You know that no other woman
would be standing at the finish. She won't let up

in the ring tonight. She trades a good punch at the end.
Her dark eyes, how they follow you in this room—
she won't let up. She's standing at the finish, both of you
still punching holes through each other & calling it love.

IT WAS JUST AN OPENING

that's all it was

        just fighting

out of my head

        doing whatever

it took to reach him

      there was no real plan

it was whatever it took

       fighting him was it

all fighting no head

     just to reach that's all

no head just doing

       my plan fighting

to reach out of my head

      fighting to reach him

doing it took my all

       fighting my all out

that's whatever it took

      to reach an opening

ROUND 11

On November 16, 1979, Bobby Chacon fought Alexis Argüello of Nicaragua, in a highly anticipated bout televised broadly throughout the Americas. Chacon lost in the seventh round by referee technical decision.

you take your wife's clothes off

muy franco con las manos abajo

you've forgotten the shape of her belly

Chacon logra conectar bien

blood fresh from your face stains sheets

está bajando demasiado la derecha

the only woman who will love you after a loss like that

Argüello hay que boxearle con mucha inteligencia

you hear her whisper

Bobby Chacon demasiado valiente

let's get out of the valley, move north to the country

comió demasiado, tomó demasiado, se infló

you know she's tired of fighting

agasajado por todas partes

she wants the fresh air you promised

eso fue lo principio del fin para Bobby Chacon

her eyes two wells you can't climb out of

empezó ahí Argüello a soltarse

twenty acres in Palermo, open fields & sun

Chacon está sangrando profusamente

yes, you give in, whatever you want

no puede responder a la campana Bobby Chacon

SHE SAID, HE SAID

she wanted me
to get out
of boxing & I
wanted to get out
but I went to
Sacramento to get
ready to fight
we talked
on the phone
we argued
she wanted out
& I wanted
boxing
& I went
to Sacramento
we argued
on the phone
we talked
she wanted me
to get out
of Sacramento
& I wanted
to get out
of boxing
but I went
to get ready
to fight
she argued
& I argued
I went
to Sacramento
to get out
of boxing
& she went

to Sacramento
to get me out
of boxing
& we argued
I wanted to
get out but
I wanted
to fight

IN THE OLD DAYS

in the old days

I moved so

you couldn't hit me

in the ring

now I fight off the ropes

one thing I do better

depend on head movement

I move my body now

to get away from punches

my legs aren't the same

I moved so

in the old days

in the ring

you couldn't hit me

one thing I do better

now I fight off the ropes

I move my body now

depend on head movement

my legs aren't the same

to get away from punches

ROUND 12

Valorie Valorie

love

money the fame the drugs the title the glory the cars the women the money the fame the drugs the title the glory the cars the women the money the fame the drugs the title the glory the cars the women the money the fame the drugs the title the glory the cars the women the money the fame the drugs the title the glory the cars the women the money the fame the drugs the title the glory the cars the women the money the fame the drugs the title the glory the cars the women

PREDICAMENT

I've done a lot of fighting
  from Inglewood to Sacramento
    I knocked out the first guys I faced
  in two rounds or less
but the chin don't hurt
  Val she's tired of being a boxer's wife
    she's always on me about it
  the bruises & the cuts
& boxing
  I have to get it out of my blood
    I hope she doesn't
  get mad at me
I know she won't

   /

    I know she won't
  get mad at me
I hope she doesn't
  I have to get it out of my blood
    & boxing
  the bruises & the cuts
she's always on me about it
  Val she's tired of being a boxer's wife
    but the chin don't hurt
  in two rounds or less
I knocked out the first guys I faced
  from Inglewood to Sacramento
    I've done a lot of fighting

VALORIE

she looks in the mirror at her mouth in the mirror

enough it's me or the boxing it's me or the ring her mouth

in the mirror moves hardly enough it's me & the kids

or it's boxing she pleads to no one in the mirror enough

mouth hardly moving it's me or the boxing enough I'll leave

she pleads it's boxing or me or me & the kids no more

boxing enough please her mouth in the mirror it's me

it's me & the kids enough no more no more please

THE FACTS

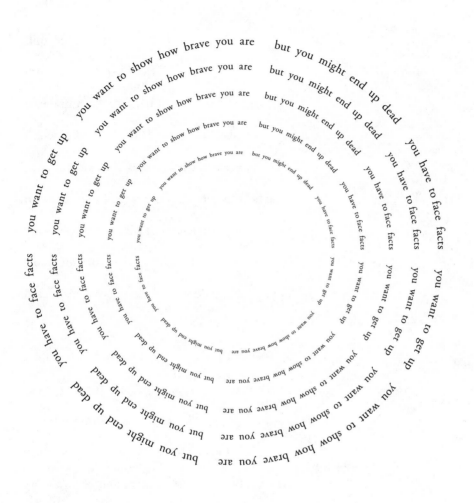

VALORIE

something   like prayer spills

from her   mouth

cup hands   around ears

cusp of   [listen]   herself

voice like prayer   she can't unlisten

the body wants   what the mind tells it to

what the husband   tells her

to   [listen]   what does she know

but slamming doors   what his breath

the heat & stale   limp her body

[listen]   his hands around her

neck reaching   [listen]   for something

like love   from his body

a kiss   when the door opens

not his breath   opening to another woman's

lips   open a mouth

to crawl inside of   all fours

skinnedkneesinching

toward throat   then up

[listen]

then out

VALORIE

[listen]

[listen]

[listen]

[listen]

skinnedkneesinching

[listen]

SHE WANTED LOVE

she thought no one loved
her she wanted me to sit
down & love her she
wanted me to love her
she loved me & she
wanted me she wanted
love to sit down she
loved love & she thought
no one loved love
thought no one thought
love she wanted no one
& she loved no one & she
thought she wanted me
to sit down & love her
love her love her love

VALORIE

her mouth

enough   her mouth

                                   enough

                                                enough

        mouth   enough

        enough   her mouth

                       enough   please

ROUND 13

On March 15, 1982, Valorie Chacon commited suicide inside of her home in Palermo, CA.

On March 16, 1982 Bobby Chacon fought Salvador Ugalde for $6,000, winning by technical knockout in three rounds.

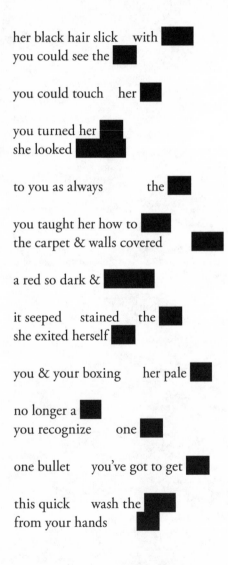

her black hair slick   with ▮
you could see the ▮

you could touch   her ▮

you turned her ▮
she looked ▮

to you as always   the ▮

you taught her how to ▮
the carpet & walls covered ▮

a red so dark & ▮

it seeped   stained   the ▮
she exited herself ▮

you & your boxing   her pale ▮

no longer a ▮
you recognize   one ▮

one bullet   you've got to get ▮

this quick   wash the ▮
from your hands

up at the gym   your ▮

children the kids ▮
& scared   their small ▮

a sadness you've never seen   ▮

in their hearts so big   one ▮
& now they're motherless ▮

everywhere   you tell them it's ▮

you don't want to ▮
react so you drive your ▮

car back to Sacramento   smell ▮

on your clothes   it's time to ▮
your challenger in the ring   your ▮

gun fists can punch a ▮

through any man   you see a ▮
you can fight your way out of or ▮

for a couple thousand   you'll ▮

even something ▮
until you see ▮

pouring out of a ▮

▮   hole   ▮   beautiful
▮   shot   ▮   blood

▮   over   ▮   face

VALORIE

go   go   there is

a   where

where   she   finds

in

her

heart

a holy feeling

THEY TOLD ME

to be **strong**

       I've got something

to cry about

       I was **strong**

yes, I cried in the ring

       yes, I was **strong**

I cried I was **strong**

       in the ring I was **strong**

they told me to cry in the ring

       I've got something

to be **strong** about

       I've got the ring

they told me

       I cry to be **strong**

to be **strong** they told me

       I cried about something

yes, I've got something

I cried, yes, in the ring

they told me I cried, yes

about something I was strong

to cry to be strong

I was about to cry in the ring

I've got to be strong

VALORIE

turn: figure,   a dream or   ill-desert—

          the stars &   nothing more   no

everything   unknown   is   the sky

               swallowed   whole   if

her name   if only   a little

MY WIFE DIED

MY WIFE DIED BECAUSE I WOULDN'T QUIT MY WIFE DIED BECAUSE I WOULDN'T

I WOULDN'T QUIT BECAUSE MY WIFE DIED I WOULDN'T QUIT BECAUSE

VALORIE

                                                              her body

                              the   wound

                              touches   touches

                                                    trying to

                                                    exist

              be

              she wants

                                            herself   whole

~~You want to forget you You will forget you You start to forget you You can't help but forget you You've begun to forget you You started to forget you You forget what you've forgotten of you You're forgetting you~~ You forgot you ~~You want to forget you You will forget you You start to forget you You can't help but forget you You've begun to forget you You started to forget you You forget what you've forgotten of you You're forgetting you~~ You forgot you ~~You want to forget you You will forget you You start to forget you You can't help but forget you You've begun to forget you You started to forget you You forget what you've forgotten of you You're forgetting you~~ You forgot you ~~You want to forget you You will forget you You start to forget you You can't help but forget you You've begun to forget you You started to forget you You forget what you've forgotten of you You're forgetting you~~ You forgot you

VALORIE

                              a kiss

                 a   gash

     held   barely

                          of the kids

        they were kids   she

       got   into this

       & again   love

                    is to be faced:

       she knows

enough

       she knows   to keep

                  the bleed

                  under skin

[RETIRED]

we could have made it
when Val asked me
but I didn't want to
I wish I could have [   ]

when Val asked me
I wish I could have [   ]
we could have made it
but I didn't want to

but I didn't want to
we could have made it
I wish I could have [   ]
when Val asked me

I wish I could have [   ]
but I didn't want to
when Val asked me
we could have made it

we could have made it
I wish I could have [   ]
when Val asked me
but I didn't want to

but I didn't want to
when Val asked me
we could have made it
I wish I could have [   ]

I wish I could have [   ]
we could have made it
but I didn't want to
when Val asked me

when Val asked me
but I didn't want to
I wish I could have [   ]
we could have made it

I wish I could have [   ]
when Val asked me
we could have made it
but I didn't want to

when Val asked me
we could have made it
but I didn't want to
I wish I could have [   ]

we could have made it
but I didn't want to
I wish I could have [   ]
when Val asked me

but I didn't want to
I wish I could have [   ]
when Val asked me
we could have made it

VALORIE

she

leaves slowly

her body

a delicate   song

her body

she   unmakes   whispers

into

the breeze

like   a

small

God

ROUND 15

"You're alright, Bobby. You got another day."—Richard Steele, referee
January 14, 1984

You're not the first man to think

if it weren't for boxing you'd be in jail or dead.

There will always be a kid who's the oldest—

three brothers, three sisters, their mouths to feed.

You stepped into the ring but no one told you

in three minutes you could go from a killer to a nobody.

You've lost the last of the money, the cash went down your throat,

steady & cool as Mancini's glove against your cheek.

It only takes one beating to realize you don't have many friends,

remember that your wife shot herself in the head. It's been a year,

maybe two. Your children's middle names, another memory gone,

like the sound of them calling to you from the kitchen.

Still you earned your purse in the second round & then some in the third.

You, a man a decade older than Boom Boom, arms aiming

for ghosts only you could see. For a moment,

the ropes against your back your sole reprieve, how you smiled—

the nick below your eye spouting blood onto the canvas—

when the referee came between those deadly fists & your broken body.

VALORIE

his   hands

boyish

her cheeks   the color

tender   now

the soul

between   them

will

break

DEFENSE

Chacon was stripped of the superfeatherweight championship title by the World Boxing Council after violating rules to a timely defense of his title against Hector Camacho.

only criminals
fight for money

    are committed
    to get enough

        to this thing to get money
        to serve seven years

            & I've paid
            the kids

                & I didn't have the money
                for my crimes

if I didn't have
to get money

    to serve
    my family

        I'd fight
        for the money

            another ten years
            I paid for my crimes

the only reason
I paid

    I'm still in this thing
    my family & my fight

        another ten years
        is to get enough money

            for the kids
            & I'm committed

VALORIE

        because

                she hears

                she ought to   fight

                  when

                  she's found in him

                  everything

ALTHOUGH THERE COULD ALWAYS BE HECTOR CAMACHO

if	~~fight~~
I	~~money~~
was	~~last~~
smarter	~~my~~
I	~~be~~
could've	~~could~~
been	~~this~~
done	~~&~~
by	~~secure~~
now	~~financially~~
&	~~be~~
be	~~&~~
financially	~~now~~
secure	~~by~~
&	~~done~~
this	~~been~~
could	~~could've~~
be	~~I~~
my	~~smarter~~
last	~~was~~
money	~~I~~
fight	~~if~~

VALORIE

she is

quietly

one

& poof

there there

on her bedroom floor

the

world   scatters

PUNCH-DRUNK

"What is achieved by such as this?"
—Howard Cosell

1. *Cause:*

From April 17, 1972, to June 2, 1988, Bobby Chacon boxed 67 bouts, a total of 431 rounds, with a record of 59 wins (47 by way of knockout), 7 losses (5 by way of knockout), 1 no contest.

2. *Mechanism:*

loss   of   neurons   collection

    of senile plaques   scarring   of brain tissue

attenuation   in the corpus   callosum

    neurofibrillary   tangles   damaged

cerebellum   cavum   septum   pellucidum

3. *Symptoms:*

The man looks older than he is.
The man acts older than he is.
The man can't walk in a straight line.
The man's as unsteady as fighter against the ropes.
The man lacks coordination.
The man slurs his words.
The man slurs his words.
The man slurs his words like a drunk in the morning.

The man knows he has a problem.
The man doesn't know how to fix the problem.
The man can't remember the date.
The man can't remember his mother's name.
The man can't remember where he was when his wife shot herself in the head.
The man slurs his words.
The man's lips tremble.
The man's hands tremble.
The man trembles.
The man trembles.
The man trembles.
The man will die trembling.

NOTES

The title of this book is taken from the article "Fighting Is Like a Wife" by Ralph Wiley, *Sports Illustrated*, July 11, 1983, issue. This book is written with immense gratitude and respect for Mr. Wiley, and in dedication to his memory.

This book also owes a great deal to Bernard Goldberg's HBO *Real Sports* piece on Bobby Chacon and Danny Lopez, which aired in December 2001.

All poems in the voice of Bobby Chacon are direct manipulations of quotes from the boxer taken from articles and interviews both in print and video.

"Excerpts from a Post-Fight Interview: Bobby Chacon Lives for Tomorrow" is after "Excerpts from an Interview with Metta World Peace aka Ron Artest aka the Pandas Friend" by Eve L. Ewing, *Electric Arches* (Haymarket, 2017).

"Valorie [because he keeps a knife]" borrows from "The Only Fault" by Rachael Yamagata, "the only fault I'll take from you / is how you run from what you wish to keep."

"Valorie [striking with his enormous grin]" borrows from "The Only Fault" by Rachael Yamagata, "if it remained unclear / between the two of us / which one would be the one to break the other's heart" (*Elephants . . . Teeth Sinking Into Heart,* Warner Bros./Wea, 2008).

"Round 3" is after "Freedom" by Tyehimba Jess, *leadbelly* (Wave, 2005).

"Round 4" is written in memory of Santos Rodriguez.

"Round 6" lines are taken from commentary on various Chacon fights throughout his career.

"Round 8" repurposes the line "and now they're both in pain, but they keep each other company, in a way," from the play *The Way West* (2014) by Mona Mansour, to whom the poem is dedicated. Thank you, Mona.

The epigraph in "Round 15," "You're alright, Bobby. You can have another day," was spoken to Chacon by referee Richard Steele after he stopped the bout one minute seventeen seconds into the third round, calling a win by referee technical decision for Ray "Boom Boom" Mancini.

CITATIONS

American Broadcasting Company (ABC). *Wide World of Sports.* "WBC World Super Featherweight Championship: Bazooka Limón vs. Bobby Chacon." Aired December 11, 1982, in broadcast syndication, ABC.

Fox Deportes Boxeo. "Alexis Argüello vs. Bobby Chacon." Aired November 16, 1979, in broadcast syndication, Fox Deportes.

Gumble, Bryant. *Real Sports with Bryant Gumbel.* Season 7, episode 2. Reported by Bernard Goldberg. Aired December 11, 2001, in broadcast syndication, HBO Sports.

HBO Sports. *World Championship Boxing.* "Ray Mancini vs. Bobby Chacon." Aired January 14, 1984, in broadcast syndication, HBO Sports.

Johnson, Roy S. "Bobby Chacon Can't Stop Fighting." *New York Times,* June 17, 1982.

Katz, Michael. "A Loose Chacon Learns to Face the Facts." *New York Times,* January 13, 1984.

———. "Plays; The Power of a Feint in the Ring." *New York Times,* May 17, 1983.

New York Times. "Misfortune Continues to Follow Chacon." May 15, 1983.

Putnam, Pat. "Chacon Was from Hunger." *Sports Illustrated,* June 30, 1975.

Roberts, Sam. "Bobby Chacon, Boxing Champion Hounded by Misfortune, Dies at 64." *New York Times,* September 10, 2016.

Wiley, Ralph. "Fighting Is Like a Wife." *Sports Illustrated,* July 11, 1983.

ACKNOWLEDGMENTS

Thank you to the editors of the following journals and magazines, where some of these poems first appeared (sometimes in slightly different versions or with different titles): *Barrelhouse, Boulevard, Gulf Coast, Kenyon Review, Pinwheel, Ploughshares,* the *Rumpus, Southern Indiana Review,* and *Triangle House.*

My deep gratitude for the fellowships provided by MacDowell and Vermont Studio Center, where many of the poems were made and remade.

I am indebted to many teachers, readers, and friends along the way—for reminding me why we create when I most need to be reminded, for bringing me back to myself, for pushing me to pursue surprise on the page and off, and for encouraging me to make from a place of love and community—thank yous will never suffice, and yet: thank you.

To the Coffee House Press team: thank you. Erika Stevens, editor extraordinaire: thank you.

I would be nowhere without the love and support from my family. All my words are to for because of you.

Coffee House Press began as a small letterpress operation in 1972 and has grown into an internationally renowned nonprofit publisher of literary fiction, essay, poetry, and other work that doesn't fit neatly into genre categories.

Coffee House is both a publisher and an arts organization. Through our *Books in Action* program and publications, we've become interdisciplinary collaborators and incubators for new work and audience experiences. Our vision for the future is one where a publisher is a catalyst and connector.

LITERATURE
is not the same thing as
PUBLISHING

FUNDER ACKNOWLEDGMENTS

Coffee House Press is an internationally renowned independent book publisher and arts nonprofit based in Minneapolis, MN; through its literary publications and *Books in Action* program, Coffee House acts as a catalyst and connector—between authors and readers, ideas and resources, creativity and community, inspiration and action.

Coffee House Press books are made possible through the generous support of grants and donations from corporations, state and federal grant programs, family foundations, and the many individuals who believe in the transformational power of literature. This activity is made possible by the voters of Minnesota through a Minnesota State Arts Board Operating Support grant, thanks to the legislative appropriation from the Arts and Cultural Heritage Fund. Coffee House also receives major operating support from the Amazon Literary Partnership, Jerome Foundation, McKnight Foundation, Target Foundation, and the National Endowment for the Arts (NEA). To find out more about how NEA grants impact individuals and communities, visit www.arts.gov.

Coffee House Press receives additional support from Bookmobile; Dorsey & Whitney LLP; Elmer L. & Eleanor J. Andersen Foundation; Fredrikson & Byron, P.A.; the Matching Grant Program Fund of the Minneapolis Foundation; Mr. Pancks' Fund in memory of Graham Kimpton; the Schwab Charitable Fund; and the U.S. Bank Foundation.

THE PUBLISHER'S CIRCLE OF COFFEE HOUSE PRESS

Publisher's Circle members make significant contributions to Coffee House Press's annual giving campaign. Understanding that a strong financial base is necessary for the press to meet the challenges and opportunities that arise each year, this group plays a crucial part in the success of Coffee House's mission.

Recent Publisher's Circle members include many anonymous donors, Patricia A. Beithon, Anitra Budd, Andrew Brantingham, Dave & Kelli Cloutier, Mary Ebert & Paul Stembler, Jocelyn Hale & Glenn Miller, the Rehael Fund-Roger Hale/Nor Hall of the Minneapolis Foundation, Randy Hartten & Ron Lotz, Dylan Hicks & Nina Hale, William Hardacker, Kenneth & Susan Kahn, Stephen & Isabel Keating, the Kenneth Koch Literary Estate, Cinda Kornblum, Jennifer Kwon Dobbs & Stefan Liess, the Lambert Family Foundation, the Lenfestey Family Foundation, Sarah Lutman & Rob Rudolph, the Carol & Aaron Mack Charitable Fund of the Minneapolis Foundation, Gillian McCain, Malcolm S. McDermid & Katie Windle, Mary & Malcolm McDermid, Daniel N. Smith III & Maureen Millea Smith, Peter Nelson & Jennifer Swenson, Enrique & Jennifer Olivarez, Alan Polsky, Robin Preble, Jeffrey Sugerman & Sarah Schultz, Nan G. Swid, Grant Wood, and Margaret Wurtele.

For more information about the Publisher's Circle and other
ways to support Coffee House Press books, authors, and activities,
please visit www.coffeehousepress.org/pages/donate or
contact us at info@coffeehousepress.org.

Fighting Is Like a Wife was designed by
Bookmobile Design & Digital Publisher Services.
Text is set in Adobe Garamond Pro.